How to Become

a

Best-Selling Author

Using Powerful but
Easy–to–Make Videos

By Karen MacMurray
http://www.promote-your-book.com

Creative Endeavors Publishing

Published by Creative Endeavors Publishing

1011 Calhoun St. Monroe, NC 28112

www.creativeendeavorspublishing.com

ISBN: 13 978-1492181910

ISBN: 10-1492181919

Printed in the United States of America

Cover design by Karen MacMurray

Your Free Gift

I want to thank you for your purchase of this book. I want to offer you a free report that is exclusive to my readers.

One of my goals is to empower other writers. That is why I wrote **"WordPress Plugins for Writers."** We have requirements that Internet Marketers don't have. I hope it facilitates your success. You can download it at www.promote-your-book.com/gift

Dedication

To all the writers who dream of becoming

a best-selling author.

Table of Contents

INTRODUCTION

Like many of you, I too belong to writers' groups where there are people who can write rings around me. Many of my friends have produced wonderful, interesting, and well-written books, yet have little to show for their efforts monetarily. You are the reason behind this book. My curiosity about how to "make things happen" and my compulsion to research, then put into practice what I learn has resulted in this ebook. Doing everything in this book may seem daunting at first, but if you tackle it in bite-sized pieces, you will eventually get to the point where the cash will come to you in increasing amounts.

Unless you have a contract with a leading publisher that has the time, expertise, and money to promote your book, you have to do all the marketing and promoting yourself. What you will learn from this ebook will give you a huge advantage over your competition. There will be work involved, but I think you will find the actual makings of videos are fun and surprisingly easy. After that, you are going to learn how to leverage them like crazy.

A little about me; I am a librarian, an author, and information junkie. I have been writing for years and published books, magazine and newspaper articles, book reviews, and won a few writing contests. Marketing has always fascinated me, and I have paid to be mentored by most of the big names in the world of Internet Marketing.

Why am I putting such an emphasis on videos, the internet, and leveraging? I need to give you some facts of life. As I am sure you all know, Google is the number 1 search engine in the world. I suspect you know who or what is second – yes, it is YouTube! YouTube has

almost as many searches as Google itself.
Google loves media, and Google just happens to
own YouTube. I was listening to a podcast
recently and heard Kim Garst put out some
interesting statistics. She said that 90% of all
information to the brain is visual, that 65% of
people learn visually, and we retain 80% of what
we see. In addition to this, over 4 billion people
view YouTube every day. That is over 140 views
for every man, woman, and child on earth!
Wow, not to use video to promote your book is
to be left behind at the starting gate!

Videos are the fastest way to get your
product or book on the first page of Google,
especially when you learn how to do so in a few
steps. It is time for a little honesty on my part.
What you learn here can get you on that first
page, but it isn't going to keep you there. I will
go into that later, but the video is the first and
most important part of your strategy. Ninety-

nine percent of what you will learn here will be free.

The information here can be used by fiction and nonfiction authors as well as anyone wanting to promote something. Some of the techniques and types of videos will be geared toward one or the other. You will have to decide whether to use some or not.

First, what kind of person are you? Are you creative, a storyteller, the analytical type, the romantic type? Ninety-nine percent of all videos on YouTube (and other video sites) are made by amateurs, so don't feel it will probably be too much for you. Your first video won't be as good as your second or third, but it is easy to catch on.

I recommend that you go to YouTube and search for book trailers. You should see a variety of kinds – live action (those are usually made by the professionals), images with words, cartoon, talking heads, collage, demonstrations, and more. I want you to get some kind of an idea of the look you want for your first video.

A website called "Circle of Seven" does a lot of action videos for authors. Most of those will be beyond you; but if you are considering paying to have one made, I think they start around $1,000.00.

Types of Videos

- Full face or Interview (author interviews or reading the first chapter of your book).

- Demonstration of a product or process (for the nonfiction author).

- Slide show with PowerPoint or Prezi (you can include animation, music, voice-over, text-over, images).

- Split screen (image of your book cover + slides or narration, can also be a video article).

- Screen capture (for nonfiction authors, demonstrating a digital product).

- Collage of images being added one after another with or without text, animation).

- Cartoon (PowToon is a free program that creates moving cartoons).

- Drawing on the screen while talking (probably nonfiction authors, unless you are inventive and somewhat of an artist).

The easiest type of video for you depends on your personality, but the slide show format is my favorite. The Full face or Interview type is the quickest to make if you feel comfortable seeing yourself on video and comfortable with the process.

Mostly Free Video Recording Software

I've used a number of free video recording software as well as paid software and have found they all have pluses and minuses to them. In addition, there are probably three or four new programs coming out all the time.

If you are a perfectionist or doing live-action, there are cheap video editing programs available such as PowerDirector. Editing programs allow you to cut out visual and auditory mistakes, fade images in-and-out, and just make your video look more professional. The negative about using these is not the cost, but the time it takes to actually correct things. I think it is easier to just record it again.

The ones I will be telling you about are the ones that have good reviews and that I personally like because they are easy or they have some feature I like to use. Whichever one you select, you will be able to find tutorials on YouTube to shorten your learning curve.

- Windows Live Movie Maker
- Photo Story 3
- Jing Project
- PowerPoint
- Screencast-O-Matic
- ActivePresenter

Windows Live Movie Maker

This is one of the first video capture programs I used. It comes free with your computer. Sometimes I upload something I recorded elsewhere into Windows Live Movie Maker. You can clip and trim the images and rotate the video. Recording with your webcam and easy upload to YouTube makes this a good basic program. A lot of schools have their students use this for class projects.

Cons: When I upload a slide show from PowerPoint, it doesn't keep any of the animation; no voice-over and some of the advanced icons can be confusing. It only saves in one format – WMV, but I go to my favorite file conversion program – Zamzar and convert it to something else more friendly like MP4 or FLV.

Photo Story 3

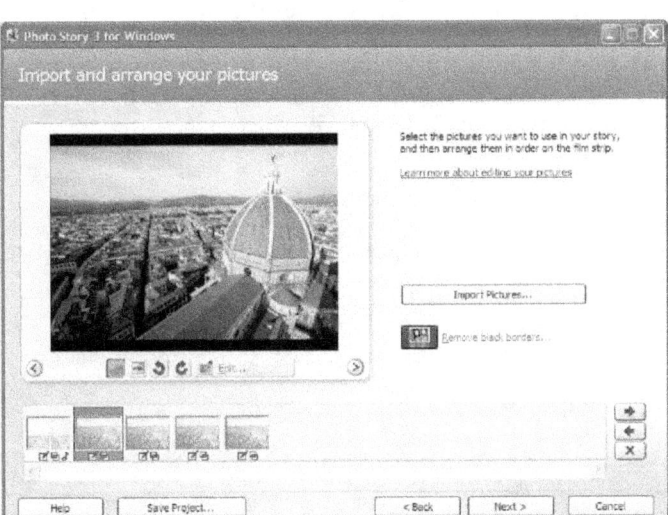

I really like this free program. It received 4 stars from CNET editors, showing that the reviewers like it too. It has some great features that the others don't have. You simply put your images in and arrange them in the order you want. You can pan, fade in-or-out, remove black edges, narrate, or add music. It also has a "Create Music" section where you can create original music by selecting various instruments, speed, atmosphere, etc. You will have original music without the fear of getting a virus or sued. The music fades in at the beginning and out at the last slide. It only has one format, but again, www.Zamzar.com is out there.

Cons: You can't import other video or slides with other animation from PowerPoint.

Jing Project

This is one of the easiest free programs to use for screen capture. The editing is only basic: Adding arrows, text, frame, and highlighting. It provides a free account with Screencast, and you can keep your video private or make it public as well as upload to video directories. You have to add your music and narration as you record, and there isn't any editing. You can upload it to Windows Live Movie Maker or an editing program and correct things. I think of this as a "quick and dirty" video creation tool.

Cons: You are limited to 5 minutes, but you should keep your video to 1 ½ minutes and certainly no longer than 3 minutes. Viewers often stop watching if you go longer than 3 minutes. Whichever type of video you make, you should put a "call to action" at the end or reinforce the book or product you are selling. You have to add your music and narration as you record, and there isn't any editing.

Screencast-O-Matic

I am hearing more and more positive comments from friends who use this program. It is good for doing demonstrations, and the free version allows 15 minutes of recording. It can capture the webcam on your computer, and it does embed a watermark to the video. The recordings are easily uploaded to YouTube or Screencast-O-Matic, and you have a variety of formats to save to. This program has been recommended by teachers who think the free version is better than any other free tool, except ScreenFlow (Mac) and Camtasia ($300.00). This is a more advanced Jing Project.

Cons: The Pro version is $15.00 a year, but has editing tools and additional features.

PowerPoint

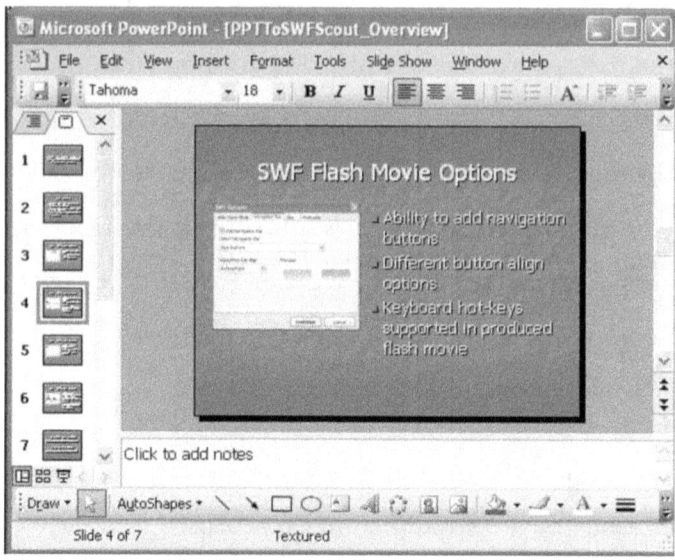

This is one of my favorite programs because you can do so much with it. PowerPoint can have a bit of a learning curve, so YouTube tutorials will come in handy. The animation is easy and fun to put in. Adding movies or other videos is not difficult. Sometimes adding sound is difficult. I have learned to print out the instructions about adding sound and follow them religiously. I forget from one video to another how to add the music and/or voice-over, but it is worth it! You can indicate how quickly or slowly a slide comes up, and they have transition styles to pick from. One of the best features is the ability to push a button to turn it into a video! I have PowerPoint 2007, so I put the file on a flash drive and take it to the library, where they have 2010, and push that button.

Cons: Be sure to keep all your files, including sound in one file, or you will have problems in this area. It costs money to buy, but again, the library is available.

ActivePresenter

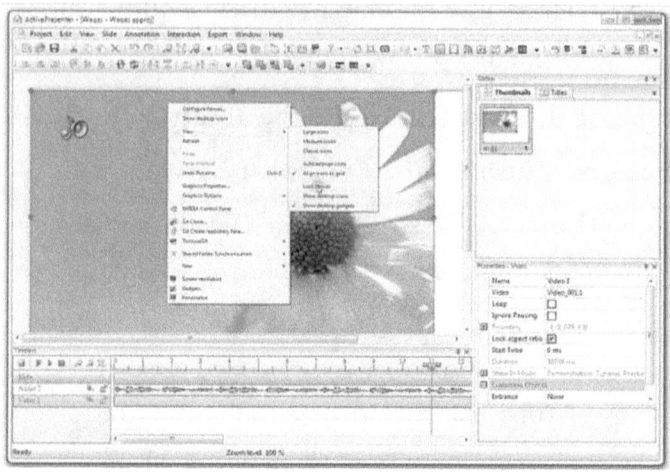

One of the most powerful video creation programs without a watermark or a time limit. You can download their PDF manual, which is a nice plus. There are 3 versions, but the free one has a lot of features: Capture screenshot, you have a choice of 4 video formats, you can insert annotation such as shape, text, highlighting, timeline, spotlights, and closed caption. Their sidebar has thumbnails like PowerPoint and Windows Live Movie Maker. This program got 4 ½ stars on www.download.cnet.com.

Getting Started

The first thing you have to do is create some kind of outline on how you are going to proceed. Like any book, you have to start with a hook to capture your audience's attention and to hold them until you leave them with wanting to know more or what is next.

I recommend you watch some book or product trailers and figure out for yourself what you like about them, and with the ones that weren't very good, why. If you are a nonfiction author, you will probably start with some kind of a problem. Fiction writers can use this as well, but you will need to start to build your character as well. How did you begin your book?

I pulled some books off my shelf and looked at the first pages. A Dick Francis novel, *Forfeit,* started with "The letter from Tally came on the day Bert Checkov died." Wow, I can see that in my mind! Robert Tanenbaum's book, *Absolute Rage's* first line is "Killing people is so easy that the iron laws of supply and demand make it hard to earn a decent living doing it."

In the nonfiction arena, I grabbed an old Wayne Dyer book that started with "Look over your shoulder. You will notice a constant companion. For want of a better name, call him Your-Own-Death."

Another nonfiction book, *The Right Way to Write, Publish and Sell Your Book,* by Patricia Fry, starts out "More people today than ever before are becoming authors. Unfortunately, most of them fail in their quest for success." Ouch!

All of these would be great starters for a book trailer. You have a short period of time to grab your viewer's interest, and a great starting line is the most important piece of writing you need to do. Use all your senses, action words, and talent to build to your crescendo, and then, leave them hanging, wanting for more.

How do you add suspense, ambiance, and anticipation? First, it will be by your choice of words. You move on from the outline to a written narration. Read the narration out loud and notice where you need to include extra time to add tension and pacing. Time yourself. For a minute and a half video, you will probably use a dozen images unless your book is an action thriller, or you want to create a special effect with product attributes. What do you see your images looking like? Are they of people, nature, or action scenes?

Video Attributes

Images

You have your narration down and have timed it. The next steps are the images. You can use photographs, live videos, graphics, or a combination of these. I like to use a storyboard. You can get a copy of the storyboard I use at www.promote-your-book.com/resources. I also use PowerPoint. I add three blank slides, then go to Print and select Handouts and select 3 to a page. It will give you 3 large images with generous lines to put the narration.

Where do you get your images? Be careful about using other people's images without their permission. You can get free images from "Creative Commons." The Creative Commons is places where people offer their pictures or images and illustrations for free, but usually ask for some kind of comment or attribute in your work as to where it comes from. Flickr and the Gutenberg Project are two places you can get images.

You can also purchase "royalty-free" images from places such as www.istockphotos.com, www.shutterstock.com, and other similar sites. If you Google royalty-free or copyright-free images, many will come up to look through.

I have a list of free photograph sites at www.promote-your-book.com/resources. The copyright law states that you can use something from a book or collection as long as it is not more than 10% or "the essence" of the material. You can legally take a piece of something and use it. For instance, I once took the back of a man's head and upper coat and put it in front of a picture of a ship sailing away. This represented a jilted man watching the ship his fiancé sailed off in to escape marriage to him.

Think outside the box with this and you can come up with useful images of quality. For example, I have seen a book trailer about a romantic book that panned very slowly across a Victorian room that created a great ambiance.

I've also seen a slow pan up a woman's dress, but the scene stopped; we saw more than her shin, so the subject was not identifiable. In another video, we only saw the back of a person, yet it conveyed everything it needed to.

I have taken a woman's face and given her different hair and masculine clothes (my heroine was passing as a man). You can also put different images together in a graphics program, flip them, rearrange them, and make a "collage," so to speak – which is new, original, and legal.

Your YouTube Image

The image that comes up when someone searches for your video is taken from the exact center of the video. This might not be easy to control, but bear it in mind. An ugly image can turn people off before they click. You can have more control of this by becoming involved with YouTube's Partner Program, which involves advertising before your book trailer starts. Later in this book, I will tell you about another powerful way to influence this using a plugin on your blog.

Adding Movement or Action to Your Images

Now, we are getting to the place that you have to decide which video capture software to use. All the software programs I recommended, with the exception of Jing Project, have the ability to pan and zoom. Most of them only pan up or down. Photo Story 3 can pan from a corner to the center as well. In addition, they can pan from the large image to a small section, and the reverse. In PowerPoint, you have a lot more choices. Here are some instructions, if you haven't explored that before:

1. Open PowerPoint and select the background color black.

2. Import pictures.

3. Click on the Animation tab.

4. Select "Custom Animation."

5. Click on the image and make it fit the slide.

6. Click on Add Effect in the right pane.

7. Click on Faded Zoom and/or Shrink/Grow.

8. Select slow speed and have it start "After Previous."

9. Preview.

In addition to panning and zooming, transitions are useful if used judiciously. Fading up from black at the beginning, out at the end, and when you have a major time change or scene change is useful.

Professional videographers use effects that are felt, but not glaringly obvious. For example, a historical novel book trailer I made called *My Father's Legacy,* made with Photo Story 3 – to see it, go to http://youtu.be/oUL1qL5baQE – as you will see, I have yet to finish the book, but I am building interest by letting the viewer know it is coming. You can do the same!

Other effects you might want to use include "flying in." Other images are particularly useful for product videos. In a book trailer I did for A.J. Hartley, called *The Peregrine Pact,* (to see it on YouTube, use this URL – http://youtu.be/gazPz8MYSko, I started with a picture of the boy in the center of the screen, then slowly faded in and around him several images: An image of England (where he came from), a magic mirror, a picture of the private school he was enrolled in and his friends. With this technique, I was able to create an atmosphere for the story and background information quickly and effectively. The music in that video was faded in-and-out using a free program called "Audacity." I built-up terror by quickly bringing in a scary and strange sound I found on a free music site.

In Photo Story 3, one of their effects is atmosphere on the picture. I particularly like creating the image of fog in a street scene.

Let your story determine how much movement to use. The speed of the images needs to match the character of the book. If you have time, look at some YouTube videos on PowerPoint animation to see how you can increase your overall video effect.

Adding Sound

There are basically three types of sound to consider: Music, voice-over, and special effects. There are some marketers who say that sound is even more important than the visuals.

I don't know that I agree with that, but it is certainly powerful in creating atmosphere and ambiance.

Music is usually something you have to add from outside your video unless you are using Photo Story 3. You can add music from the outside or create your own. Take a look at this screen shot from Photo Story 3.

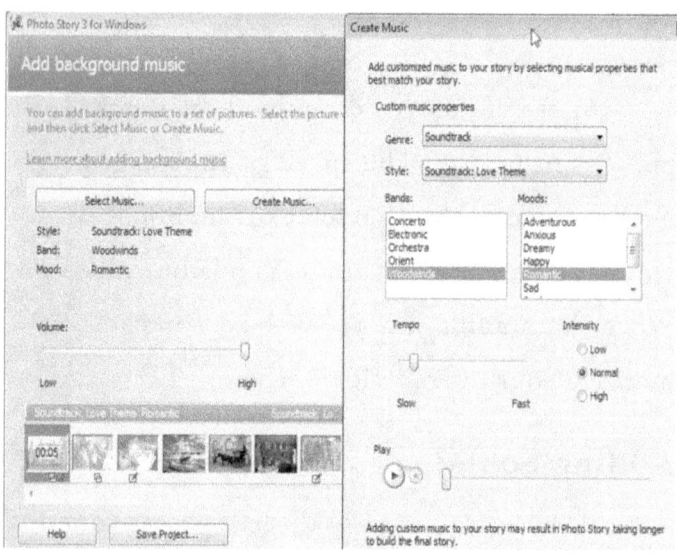

Besides being just fun to play with, you can create a wide-variety of music by varying the pace, volume, instruments, genre, and composer. The program fades it in with the first image and fades it out at the last picture.

There are websites that provide "royalty-free music" that you can use. At the back of this ebook, I will provide lists of many of those sites. A caveat – music sites online often have viruses lurking. I head off to the library with my flash drive. They have much better firewalls than I do, so I plug in my earphones and settle down to listen away.

If you find produced music that was made before 70 years ago, you are probably safe. Plus, there is the 10% rule I mentioned regarding images. Lesser-known musicians are often happy to let you use a small segment of their work, if you give them credit.

Music Loops

They are usually one to five minutes long and are royalty-free. If you go to Google and search for "Free Music Loops," you will find many results, and you only have to pay a small fee to use them. I purchased 1,000 loops for $19.00 a couple of years back. They are well-named for easy selection, and I consider them well worth the money.

If you need to change the music during the video, a free program called "Audacity" is easy to use. With that program, I was able to speed up (and increase the volume) a sound to create terror, soften it, join it with another, and time it for exactly the right moment in the video. Check out the video I mentioned earlier, called *The Peregrine Pact*.

Adding sound to PowerPoint is an area I find challenging, but doable. Here are a few tips:

- Put music, images, and sound effects in one folder

- Print out the instructions and follow them to the letter

I have used PowerPoint many times and still manage to forget a step, causing problems and my hair to turn grey. Once I printed out the instruction and followed them to the letter, it has been smooth sailing.

Sound Effects

Sound effects are easy to find and add. PowerPoint has a number built-in. This is an area that is easy to find free online as well; bells, trains, rain, bombs, oceans, birds – just about anything you can think of.

Voice-Over

Voice-over is where a narrator reads your copy as the video progresses. You can do this yourself or hire someone to do it for you. Places to look for talent are Fiverr, Elance, Freelancer, and Upwork, formerly known as O'desk. Be sure you have the narrator give you a voice sample first and they have a good track record working for others.

Text-Over

Text-over is where you type your narration over the image. The words can fade in, float across the screen from one side to the other, or whatever will create the feeling you want. Take a look at some book trailers. This is probably the most common form of providing information and usually has music softly playing in the background. All the video software, other than Jing Project, enables this feature.

How to Give Credit to Original Creators of Music or Photographs

Since your video is a flowing creation, you can give credit at the end, right after you tell your viewer where they can purchase your book. Just like in a professional film you see at the theater, you can give credit to your friends who help you and those whose images and music you utilized. Giving credit makes you look professional and trustworthy.

A Different Type of Video – Animation

Animated videos have never been so easy to create! I suspect these are most likely to be used by those writing nonfiction. You will find a list of free software programs in the Resources area of this ebook. Here are two free programs I have played around with:

PowToon

PowToon has background libraries, characters, and props. You can download your own images and animate them as well. Stick figures and plain backgrounds are the starting point. Voice-over and music can be added and pacing done using their timeline.

Moovly

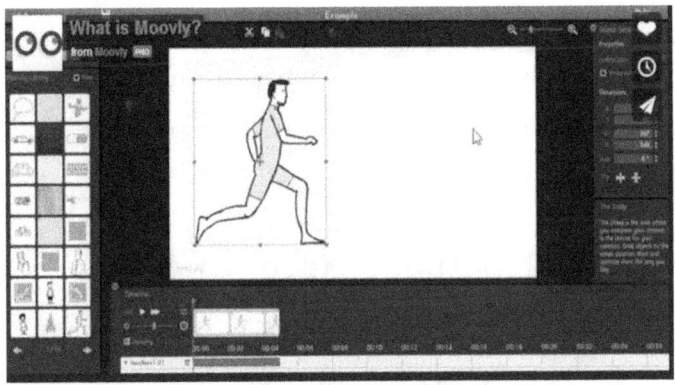

Moovly has a free account as well as paid versions. Moovly and PowToon have very different looks. In Moovly, you start by picking a style. Here are some of them.

Both animation platforms were surprisingly compelling when motion and voice were added. Take a look at some examples before deciding which one to use.

A Tip About Videos on Some Social Media Sites

Friends+Me on Google+ shares content from Google+ to other social networks by checking your Google+ business page (or personal page) at regular intervals. If posts or videos are found, they are reposted to other social networks you've associated with Friends+Me. That means less work for you!

While I am on the subject of Google+, any information you have on there seems to rank higher on Google Search than comparable information on other social media platforms. YouTube and Google are related after all.

One powerful utilization, I can see for you, is to create a simple 20- to 30-second animated video that you put on Google+ as a teaser, describing your Hangout and pointing viewers to your 1 ½-minute to 3-minute book trailer.

The Beginning and Ending of Your Video

In the Beginning

First impressions in videos are crucial. Both your image and title combine to determine whether someone clicks on it and views it. The image YouTube selects is not the one you select. It is the image that is in the exact center of your video. The title, however, is in your hands. If your book is fiction, you are going to use the title of the book. You must think about that title! Is it compelling? Does it contain high value words that create a sense of curiosity? If it doesn't, consider using something else instead.

Captivating Video Titles

I looked up the top ten titles for 2014. Here are a few of them: "Burn for Me," "Immortal Crown," "The Ascendant," "The Laughing Monsters," "Whiskey Tango Foxtrot,"

"Girl on the Train," and "Euphoria." Each one of these makes me want to know more. The website "MerchantWords" will run a search for you on your keywords (they have a free version). The title of your book does not have to be the title of your video. Some authors use their book cover to start off their book trailer, but a still image is not as compelling as action images with action words. Come up with at least three different approaches; then test it by asking friends and asking your Facebook friends to vote.

Before You Upload to YouTube

There are a few things to do before you upload your video. Have you created a blog or website for yourself or your book? That doesn't have to be a difficult thing to do. If you are new to this, consider either BlogSpot (or Blogger) or WordPress.com. Both of these platforms have wonderful tutorials in YouTube and relatively simple instructions on the site itself. Of the two, I lean toward WordPress.com. Once you know the way their dashboard works and are comfortable with it, you can, at any point, transition over to WordPress.org. The reason I recommend that route is because WordPress.org has thousands of free plugins that will make your marketing and outreach easier and more powerful. WordPress.com is free while WordPress.org requires you have a host server. The cost for that server is somewhere between $4.00 and $10.00 a month.

Now that you have your blog or website, write a few articles or posts about your book. It could be about the writing, the research you did, a poll on something, or just some good information you think your followers and friends might like to know about. Space those posts out, even if you wrote them all on the same day. There are a number of free programs that will upload your site with those articles when you want. Hootesuite and TweetDeck are two.

Next, think of something you can give your readers as a freebie. I have collected information for years on all kinds of things related to writing from many books I have read and conferences I have been through. If you are interested in it, so are others.

Offer to give your freebie to those who come to your blog and will give you their first name and email in exchange. This is called "list building." You can't put an Opt-in form on WordPress.com or Blogger.com; however, you can ask them to put the information in the comments box. If you check to view the comments before the public does, you can scoop this out and put it in an Excel file.

WordPress.com has several free plugins for collecting this information.

List building will become more and more important the more successful you become! It will be slow-going at first, but I will share with you how to make it grow later on. I started off by putting my friends' emails on the list. List building is kind of like compound interest. Once you have a list, you can communicate with those people and tell them about contests, special offers (like bundled books), or your next ebook on Kindle. Successful authors recommend that if you are a new author you offer your book for free for 3 to 5 days, on Kindle, to get reviews. Those reviews then encourage others to buy your book when you put the price back to where it belongs.

If you already have your book and its name, go to Google and type the name in with [brackets]. The brackets tell Google how many items come up with the exact same words, in that exact same order. You have to know where you come from to know if your marketing efforts are working.

If you have a book published, you need to make sure you have an author page in Amazon at "Author Central." Put a little biography of yourself, list your books, and put up a picture of you. People like to see who we are. After you put up your video to YouTube, you are going to have a link to your author page. Any links to Amazon are powerful links and kindly-looked at by Google.

The last thing to do before uploading your video to YouTube is to create a sign-in name with YouTube in your name or the name of your book. If you write a particular genre, you could create a name to connect you with that genre. For instance, if you write romances about Scottish Highlanders, you could create a name like "Highlandlassie." You are allowed 14 characters to play with. Your sign-in name is going to become a powerful worker for you. You can have more than one sign-in name with YouTube. After you have created this special sign-in, make sure you go to your blog and put this sign-in as a "keyword" so your blog gets what is known as "link juice."

Time to Upload Your Video to YouTube

You will want to maximize everything you do with your video here. I've broken down the sections for you.

Some YouTube Facts & How They Impact Google Ranking

Over 4 billion videos are viewed every single day and 60 hours of video uploaded every minute. Facebook reports that people watch over 500 years of videos on their platform every day, and they share 700 videos on Twitter each minute. I can't underestimate the power of being on YouTube (and other video sites as well).

While there are many search engines, Google is the big gorilla and the pace leader. Google decides where your blog lands on their site. They use a ranking system with 9 being the highest value and 0 the lowest. Google loves media, and the easiest way to get on the first page of Google is to use media: Videos, audio recordings, pictures, slideshows, and a combination of these. Video has the advantage of having most of those components, which is why you want to use it.

Millions of people use Google to search every hour. The first listing on page one gets about 46% of all that search traffic. The second listing gets 26%, and the third, 11%. Few people ever look at results past the second page of a Google search. This is why you want to show up there.

Your YouTube Description

Make your description clear and specific. You have around 15 seconds to keep the attention of your viewer. Your video needs to stand out from the crowd. Distinguish it from other videos. Use descriptive language in complete sentences.

Give credit where do – i.e., if you have your video set inside your local high school, give them credit. There is something called "long tail keywords." People often search using phrases of 3 words or more. Use keywords to determine more specifically what your video is about. Write a unique, descriptive, and keyword rich title and description. Add your URL's to the description. Send traffic to your other social networks and your website. Put links to those social media platforms. The maximum number of words is 980 in the description. Give a brief summary about your video, no more than a couple of paragraphs long. The description must be searchable.

If you need help finding keywords, there are two tools you can use: Google's "AdWords Keyword Tool" and YouTube's "Keyword

Suggestion Tool." Make sure to choose "exact match" when you use it. Include information about places, people, and background.

Ask your viewers for a thumbs-up, shares, and comments. Be sure to respond to the comments promptly to build a sense of community and approachableness.

Categorize

The category you put your video in is part of its description. People are more likely to rate your video highly and watch it if it is placed in the correct category. "Historical Romance" will score you more viewers than just historical or just romance.

Your YouTube Title

The title of the video is the most powerful text connected to your entire video post. Your title should be catchy and describe what your video is about. The words that appear near the beginning of the title have the most weight. Use your primary keywords there that you want to rank for. The maximum title length is 100 characters. Some experts on YouTube recommend you add a video "trigger" keyword or word that attracts attention in the search engines. Some examples are: "Review," "about," and "how to."

YouTube Links

Links are important for your description, as it is a way to promote your other videos and drive traffic to your other social media networks.

YouTube Channel

You can create a channel. You don't have to have a bunch of videos before you create your channel. Include in this channel other videos you like or related to your content. If your viewers like your video, they will probably like what you like, as well, and pick out for them on that channel.

YouTube Tags

Add 10 to 20 tags per video. Each tag should be a word or phrase that is relevant to the content of the video as well as the ways in which you predict users would discover your video. Add tags in order of importance to you.

YouTube Annotations

I think of these primarily for videos promoting products. They are a powerful way to add interactive commentary to your video. They can be used as a "call to action" on your content to encourage the viewer to follow your Twitter, Facebook, or Google+ accounts.

To add annotations, select "edit video" on the video you have already uploaded; then select the annotations tab. Next, go to the timeframe where you can scroll to the place you want to add an annotation. There are 6 different types of annotations: Bubble, Note, Title, Spotlight, Label, and Pause. The most usable one is the Note. Google is able to read the annotations, so it is another way to add to your Google rank.

Annotations are a free and easy way to expand your social following, gain greater visibility, and add an interactive element to your content. An annotation asking your viewer to subscribe to your YouTube channel is supposed to be the most successful "call to action" on YouTube.

Some Suggestions for Nonfiction Videos

- Brand your page. Using a custom background helps to create "a consistent look" to your product and channel.
- YouTube has tools to help you. Google "YouTube Photoshop Template" to access some of the goodies they offer.
- Customize your banners and layout to help customize your brand.

- Use a "call to action." People are more likely to take action or purchase your book if you ask them.

Nonfiction and Product Video Sequence

1. In the beginning of the video, let the viewer know about who you are and where else they can find you, i.e.: Facebook, Twitter, etc.

2. Tell your viewer what they will get out of watching and how long the video runs. Tell them what you are going to tell them.

3. Deliver the information or value you promised in your title.

4. Summarize what you told them; repeat the benefits of what you showed them.

5. Offer advice about the information you gave them.

6. "Call to action." Ask your viewer to do something: Like your video, share the

information, make a comment, and/or go someplace to buy more of what you are offering.

7. At the end, leave some silence to let the information sink in.

Promote Your Video

Put your video on your social networks: Twitter, Facebook, Digg, Pinterest, Facebook, Google+, your website or blog, and others. Email bloggers who write blogs on your topic and send them a link. I will go into ways to do this a little later.

Ask your viewers to LIKE your video. Include icons for the social media platforms you are connected with for easy access. It has been found that people who ask their viewers to share the video have **seven times** the traffic as those who do not.

YouTube Comments

Viewers will leave comments under your video. Respond to that feedback; it will strengthen the relationship between yourself and your viewers. It will make your viewers feel important and part of your group. You can also ask them questions to get them involved and provide direction on future projects.

YouTube Captions, Transcripts, and Subtitles

You want your video to be available to every possible viewer. Captions not only allow the hearing impaired viewers to be able to watch your video, but people from every continent and language will be able to watch your video by utilizing YouTube's "automatic translation" feature to turn it into their native language. In addition, Google can read the captions and subtitles. When you provide a transcript, you are providing the exact content of your video for search engines.

New YouTube Features

There is now an easy-to-use **Editing Tool** within YouTube. It gives you a simple option to help you edit your videos. If you need or want additional help, YouTube has a **Video Creation Marketplace**, which allows small business and brands to hire YouTube video creators, who are already publishing videos, to assist you with your project.

YouTube Social Bulletin

This is a new feature of YouTube. It allows you to post links and communicate with subscribers. When you post a new bulletin, it will appear on the homepage of all your subscribers. Every time you upload a new video, post a bulletin.

The end of the book trailer is where you are going to start leveraging your book and building your empire. This is where you want to have a picture of your book.   In addition to that, you want to tell them where they can get your book or product and give them a reason to become one of your regular readers.

Provide a "call to action" by suggesting they click on the link below in the description or going to www.yourblog.com to receive a free gift for subscribing to your email list. Why would you want to do that? By building an email list, you can let your followers or list know when you are coming out with a new book, running a special sale, having a book signing at a local book store, and many other opportunities for them and for you. Most people won't want to sign up for more email coming in, so you will need to offer them something to induce them. What can you give them? Here are a few ideas:

- The first chapter of your next book.
- A white paper on the historical background of your book (this is especially of interest to historical book authors).

- The opportunity to be notified when you are on a book tour in their state or literary events you will be speaking at.

- Notice of a special pricing for your followers.

- A list of resources on whatever subject or topic the nonfiction book is on, or a list of websites with historical information.

- A link to a podcast interview with an expert in your product's field.

How to Become a Best-Selling Author

Leveraging Your Video and Book

The days after you upload your video to YouTube, go in and find the URL they give you, copy it, and place it in your description using the Edit button, so when your video is put into video directories you will get back links.

Once you are happy with your video, you are ready to start to promote and leverage it. There is a program called "Traffic Geyser" that will put your video up on all the top video sites. You could upload your video to those same video sites yourself, but they all seem to want you to jump through a bunch of hoops; and it would take days to do the same by yourself. Traffic Geyser guarantees that your video will show up on the first page of Google. It is pricy, however, at $100.00 a month, so most of us would have to bypass this program. There is an alternative, however.

There is a program called "Fiverr" that has people that will do all kinds of things for you for $5.00. You can pay someone to get bookmarks for you, write reviews, send you traffic, and even design your book cover. In Fiverr's search box, type in "Traffic Geyser." When they come up, select someone who has a good track record and will provide you with a list of the _____.

How to Maximize Your Video on YouTube

Sign-in to YouTube with your power name. Search for videos in your subject area or niche. For example, if you write historical fiction books, you want to look for other book trailers on historical fiction. When they come up, find the videos with the most views. A high-ranking video by someone else can help your ranking. Watch their video and write a positive comment about it. Be sure to say something more than "nice movie." Your power name is now connected with a page ranking (PR) 9 video. Do this for at least ten of them. Then, go in again and find the top videos for something related to the subject of your book.

I am writing a book about a Danish immigrant, so my book trailer is going to link to sites about immigration. Again, find those high-watched videos and let some of their link juice rub off on you.

If you have a sound track for your video, record that and put it on iTunes, Podcast Alley, and other podcast sites. If you didn't have a narration, read the first chapter of your book and upload that. At the end, be sure to tell people where they can purchase the book and/or go to your website.

All of those images you used on your video can be uploaded to Flickr, Picasa, and other image sites for backlinks with a page rank of 9.

Now, take the images and put them in SlideShare programs and upload for others to see. Another page rank of 9 will be coming your way.

This next technique requires a little bit of work on your part, but it will be worth it. There are at least 5 video formats that you can use to upload your video: AVI, MP4, FLV, MOV, WMV, and some other lesser used formats such as MP3, MPG, MKV, and SWF. Take your original video and make a copy of it so that you can play with. Change the length of the video a little.

Ways to do this might be to add a screenshot of your blog, promote your next book coming out, and give credit to others who have facilitated the making of your video. Extend the length of the music or change it out, alter the title, then go to a format converter. I use Zamzar, a free program. They will email your new file to you in as few as 5 minutes; longer waits during peak business hours. You will also want to create additional sign-in names that you use with each one.

How to Stand Out in Google Search Results

If you have a blog on WordPress.org, you will want to get the free plug-in for XML sitemap from https://www.xml-sitemaps.com/. Having an XML sitemap gives Google information about the videos that are on your blog or website. Normally, your video on Pinterest, Vimeo, or Facebook would link-back to YouTube rather than your blog.

By using a video sitemap, you can index the video clips on your site and when someone sees your content on Google, there will be a little video image. When people click on that picture, they will go to your site, not YouTube.

This is huge! When you do a search for something, your eyes are automatically drawn to images and your chances of being selected are better than just having words about your video.

Planting Your Video to Get Traffic and Backlinks

At the end of this ebook, you will find a list of Video Directories, Article Directories, Podcast Directories, and Slide Show Directories. This could take some time to do yourself, so you might want to find a virtual assistant or someone from Fiverr to upload your stuff. I do recommend that you double-check their work.

Forums

Forums are a good source for promotion of your website and generator of inward links. At the bottom of each person's snippet, there is a signature. After you have provided some benefit to the forum by answering a couple of questions, they will let you put a link under your name. These are called "signature blocks," and you can link them to your website or video.

Every question you answer in a forum is listed in Google and has a page rank of 9. Use keyword rich, anchor text. Go to Google and type in your keyword or subject + forum.

Social Bookmarking

The beautiful thing about bookmarking is you only have to submit your site once and it keeps giving back!

Digg

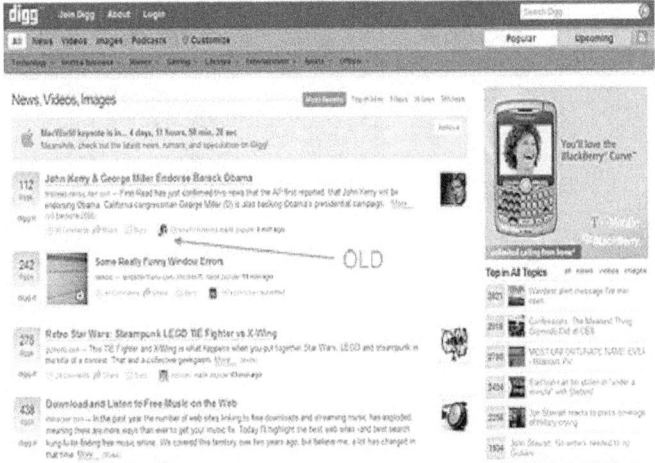

Digg is one of the biggest names in bookmarks, and they allow you to submit your website or blog. Make sure you have good information, plus your video when you do because others will see it and vote it up or down.

Your video and site can go viral if you do a good job on having some good content, good pictures, and, of course, your video embedded on your site. After you do this, email all your friends and have them start the voting.

PR 9

Reddit

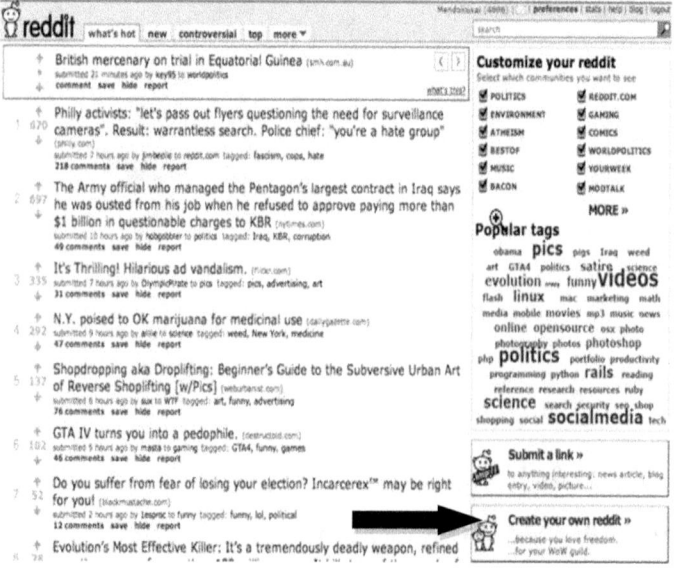

Reddit is a social networking and news service. Again, they allow you to submit your web blog, and people vote up or down. The same advice I gave you for _____ goes here as well. PR 9

Delicious

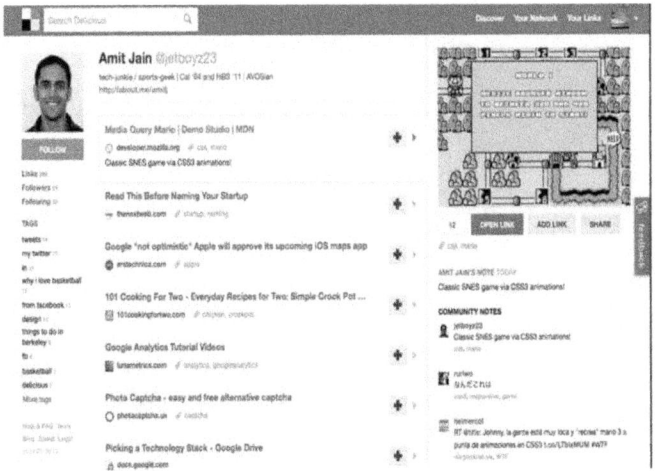

Delicious is a little different from the previous two bookmarking sites. Delicious is used for storing, sharing, and discovering bookmarks. You create stacks and categories and find others with similar interests. Use your keywords wisely and people will upload your bookmarks as well, which, of course, will include

your site and your video in a variety of places.
PR 9

StumbleUpon

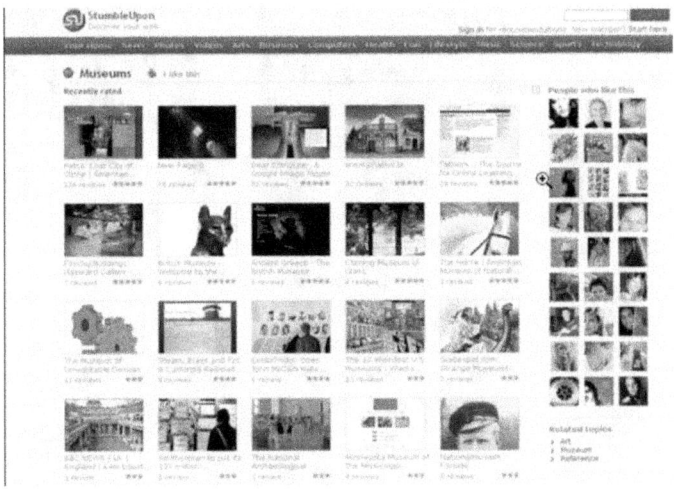

This screenshot helps you to identify what is on this site to get you a head start in figuring it out. StumbleUpon is another huge name in the world of bookmarks. It is also a discovery engine, and you want to be discovered! They help you to find what you want, follow others, and vote websites up or down. They have a toolbar for ease of use, use tagging (keywords), and you can buy traffic. PR 9

Fark

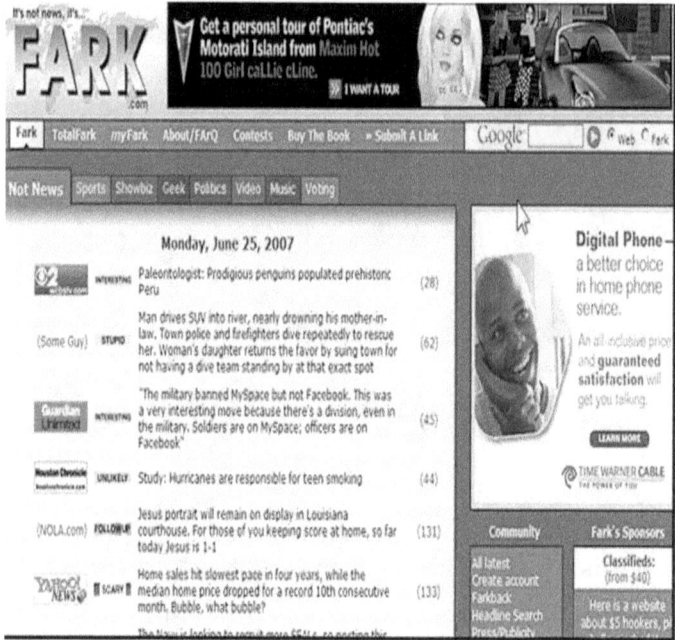

Fark is relatively new to me, but it allows you to submit your blog and video for inclusion and spreading the word about you.

Uploading Your Video to Social Media

Pinterest

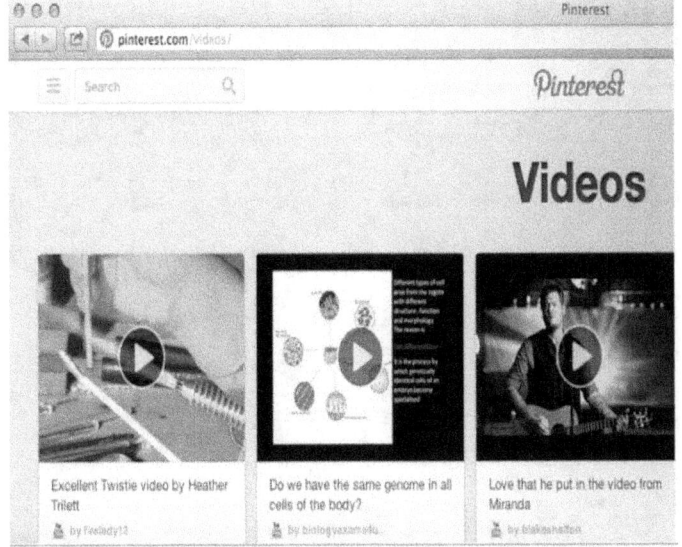

YouTube, Dailymotion, Vimeo, and other video sites will have the "Pin It" button (the red box with the white capital P). Click on it and a dialogue box will come up. Copy and paste your video's URL for the individual video site, plus your email address. Next, you will need to select the Category – Videos. You can also pin your music and your video's images.

Twitter

Go to your home page on Twitter and start a tweet. Next, go to your video and copy the URL link at the top. Now, go back to your Twitter page and paste in the URL in the box with the tweet. Click Tweet. Go to your Tweet and click on the blue link to expand the Tweet.

Click the play button to make sure everything is OK.

Facebook

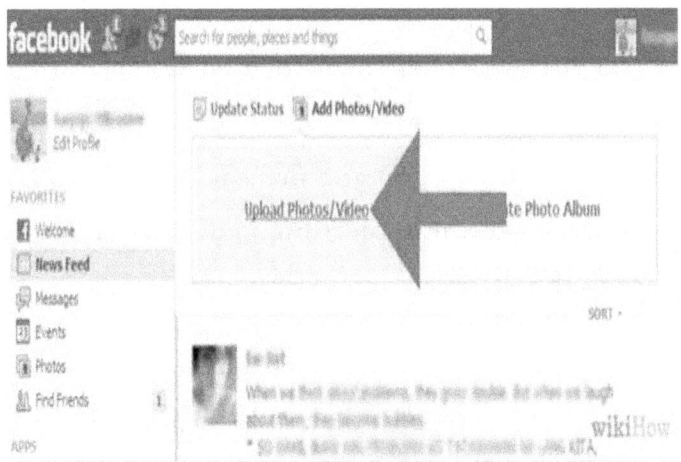

There are four ways to upload videos to Facebook. The most commonly used way is to log into Facebook. Find the blue link above the status bar that says "Add photos/videos," select a video from your computer and insert into the box that says "File Name" on your computer, click open, write a caption where it says "Say something about this video;" then click the blue Post button at the bottom right.

If you want to copy one of your friend's videos, click on the blue Share link below it; write a caption and click on the "Share Video" button.

If you want to upload a video from you smartphone, find the video and click on it, find the blue MAIL button and press it, add information to the subject box, put in your Facebook URL, and click SEND.

If you want to upload a video from YouTube, first log into Facebook then YouTube. Go to Settings and then Connected Accounts. Below that is a box with two black triangles. Find Facebook and then find the video you want; click on Share. The Facebook icon will be under the video.

Google+

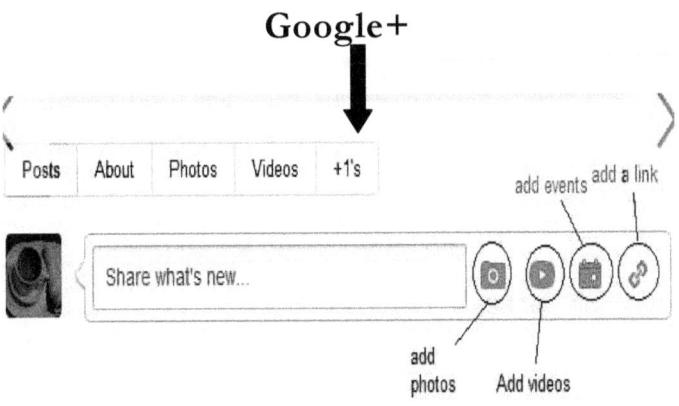

Log into your Google+ account; click on the Video tab. A box will come up with a red box that says "Upload New Video." Upload one or more videos from your computer. Choose a name; create above. When a box comes up choose Public, Family, Friends, or another one of your circles; type in a brief description about the videos. Click on the green button that says Share. People who see your video will be able to comment.

Other Forms of Promotion

Free Advertising Online

I have not used most of these sources because of time, but I hope to check them out at some time in the future.

www.CraigsList.com

www.usfreeads.com

www.walmart.oodle.com

www.backpage.com

www.recycler.com

www.classifiedadss.com

www.olx.com

www.upillar.com

www.inetgiant.com

www.50statesclassified.ca

www.stumblehere.com

www.hoobly.com

www.ablewise.com

www.webclassifieds.us

www.freeadlists.com

Paid Advertising

One Hour BackLinks

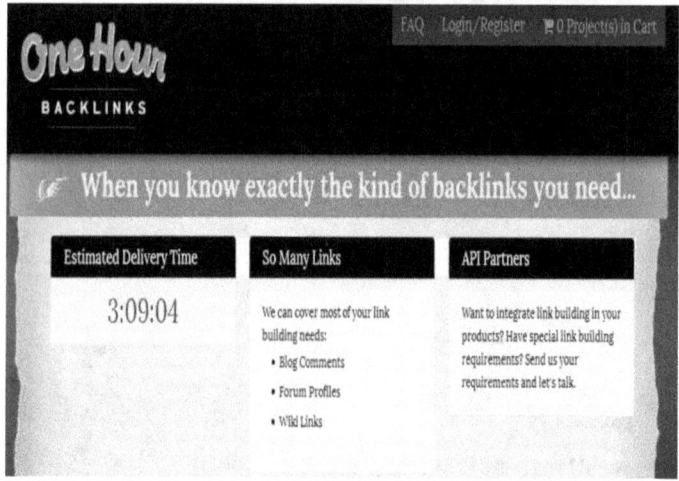

I have never used this program, but have seen it recommended a number of times by those I respect in the world of Internet Marketing.

7Search

7Search is a very economical way to advertise, and they have been around for years.

AdBrite (now SiteScout)

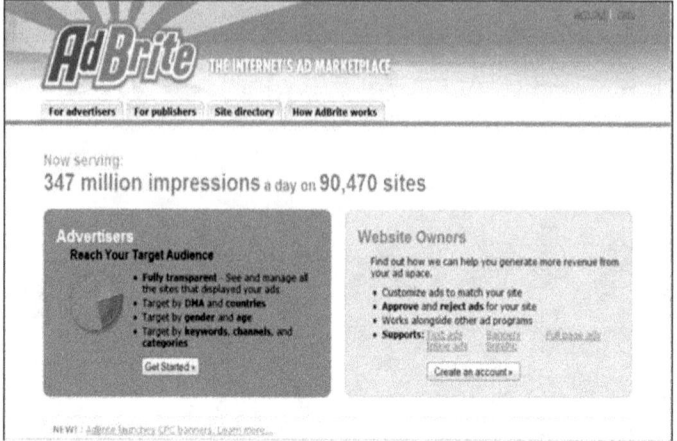

This is another economical advertising site. When I used it, it was called "AdBrite."

Google Adwords (straight commission)

This is a relatively new way to advertise on Google. It is an improvement from their previous plan because you only pay if someone actually clicks on your ad. I do recommend you keep a close eye on your account because I have learned the hard way it is wise to do so. You will be bidding on how much you pay. Google has been known to use your entire month's budget in the first week. If you decide to end your promotion with them, be very sure you go all the way to the bottom on the form (after your feedback), or you might just find yourself spending more money without realizing it.

Fiverr

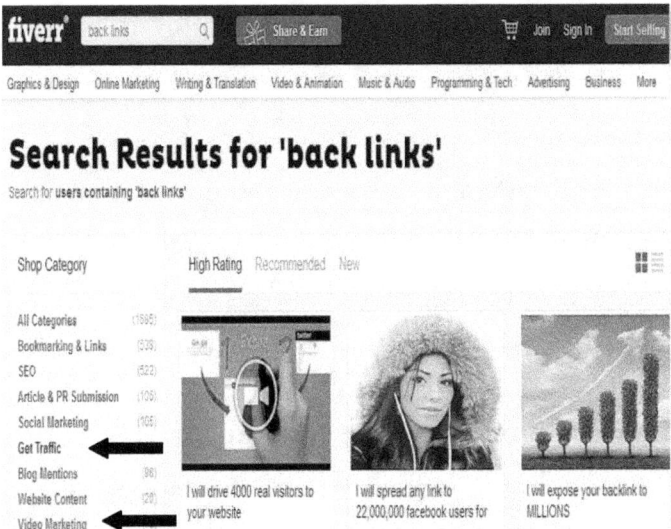

Make sure the person you choose has a good record and no major complaints. If you purchase a large number of backlinks, know that if they all go to your website you will get a Google "slap," which means you will be dead in the water for about three months. Instead have them sent to: Your YouTube video or account, your Author Page on Amazon.

Facebook Ads

Facebook ads are a mixed bag. I have heard from happy people and disappointed people. First, you must be advertising something that people who use Facebook on a regular basis might be interested in. I know that sounds logical, but it isn't to everyone. For instance, I wouldn't advertise my used car there; my newest diet secret would be a yes.

Free Promotion – Free Backlinks

Write an article for an ezine magazine. You can write about making the video, writing the book, promoting the video or book, how you developed the characters in your book, etc. The reason you want to do this is that the ezines have what is known as a Resource box at the bottom of the article. In this area you can tell people who you are and what your credentials are; however, it is far better to offer the reader some goodie on your blog. Provide them with a link to your blog, and create some kind of give away — a checklist of what you do when you write a book, the first chapter of your book, a video showing something, a quiz on their characteristics (Google for examples of quizzes you can offer). This will drive traffic to your website and in turn, increase your chances of selling your book. Ezine articles have the highest ranking (PR 6), but only allow original information. Once they have accepted it, you can then put the article in ezine directories and get lots of backlinks.

Guest Posting and Guest Podcasting

This is a great way to get backlinks and your name out there! Podcasting is ranked very high by Google. Guest posting on other bloggers is only medium-ranking, but it is still worthwhile doing. At the end of this ebook, I will provide resources for you on both of these areas.

Amazon Author Page

Amazon's Steve Scott Page

"Proven Internet Business Strategies for the Price of a Coffee"

Quality information shouldn't be expensive. The so-called 'Internet gurus' love to charge exorbitant prices; knowing this prevents many average folks from achieving success online More about Steve Scott

Bestselling Books: Make Money with YouTube - How I Made an Extra $1,187.66 from a 4-Minute YouTube Video, Email Marketing Blueprint - The Ultimate Guide to Building an Email List Asset, How to Write a Nonfiction eBook in 21 Days - That Readers LOVE!

Notice Steve's best-selling books listed on the first page.

On your Author Page, you want to put your video, a biography, and links to articles on

your blog and customer discussions. I also want to add that www.stevescottsite.com has a ton of great information about being a profitable author.

Leveraging

IMAutomator

IMAutomator has both a free and paid version. You submit the name of an article you have written and your blog or website's URL **and the article goes out to about 38 places**. Not bad for a free resource! One little problem; I keep having problems pulling up the website unless I first Google it and click on the link there.

The biggest leveraging you can get is by putting up those videos with the different formats (with a page rank of 9), and the comments you put under other peoples' videos that have large number of views and any other media (slide show, podcasts, pictures) where you can upload them.

How to Watch Your Progress

SEOquake

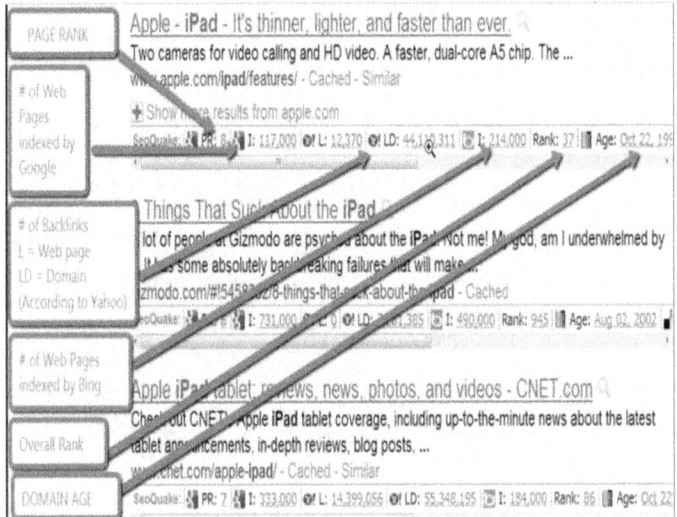

SEOquake (Search Engine Optimization) is a free plug-in for Mozilla Firefox and Google Chrome browsers. There is a "wealth of information" here, and I was glad to find this image with a breakdown of the information. Before you upload your video, type in your blog's URL and see your present Page Rank on Google. Don't be discouraged if you have a high number at first, as there are millions of websites you are competing with. You will want to come back here a week after you upload your video and a month after you upload your video and three months after you upload your video. You should see a big improvement from one week to the next! Usually it takes 3 to 6 months for most blogs to see the effects of their marketing. Using videos are different! To download SEOquake, go to www.download.cnet.com. You will also find a review there telling you a lot more than I can here.

Google Analytics

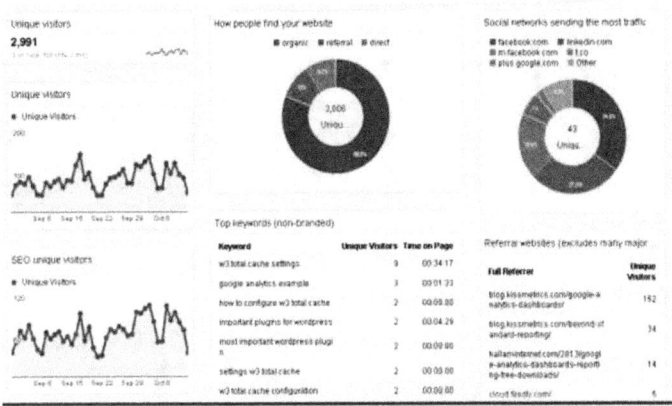

Google Analytics is free and available to you once you have registered your blog with Google. You also want to sign up for their free Webmaster tools. You can see where your visitors are coming from, when they are on your site, what keywords are pulling them in, and more. You will be able to track how your traffic and influence increases after each major leveraging project. It makes the work worthwhile!

Social Site Explorer

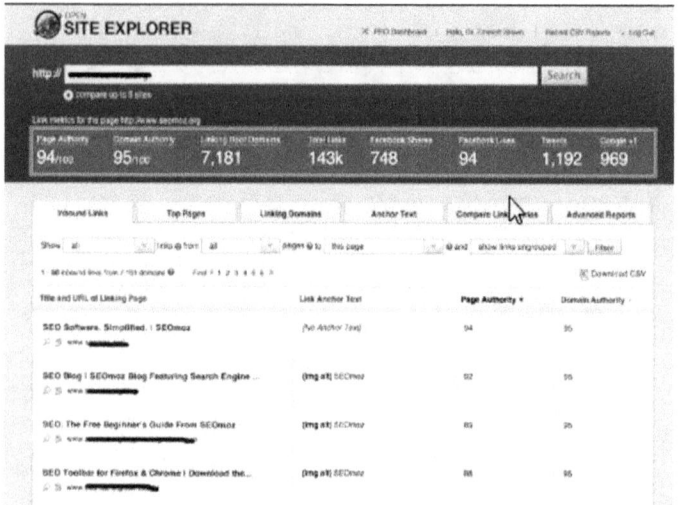

Social Site Explorer will tell you about your backlinks and followers. I like to look at my competition. If they can get a backlink from a website, I should also be able to get a backlink from them.

Recommendations

1. Put up your blog with a few articles by you and others.
2. Put up an Opt-in form to start collecting emails.
3. Create a username with your name or your book's name in YouTube.
4. Make your video.
5. Upload your video to YouTube.
6. Upload your video to Facebook.
7. Upload your video to Twitter (next day).
8. Go back into YouTube, to their Editing area and put their URL for your video into your description.
9. Look at other videos with a lot of views and leave comments.
10. Go to Fiverr and hire someone to upload your video to Traffic Geyser.
11. Create other media formats (like slideshows) from your video and upload

them to the appropriate directories, or hire someone to do it.

12. Create other videos from your original with different titles and formats.

13. Fiverr, again to have those other videos uploaded to Traffic Geyser.

14. Register your video into the Social Media Bookmark sites I mentioned. You only have to do it once, and they keep paying you with traffic.

15. Put your video on Google+ and Pinterest.

16. Do some of the free advertising sites. Craig's List has a PR 9

17. Commit to writing articles, blogging, and using Social Media a minimum of three times a week.

18. Good luck and let me know how you are doing!

Resources

All of these resources are available at
http://www.promote-your-book.com/resources.

Copyright-free music

Article Directories

Copyright-free photographs

Free Animation Software

Podcast Directories

Guest Blogging compiled by Peter Sandeen

https://soundcloud.com/infinity-loop-music
instrumental sounds

Other Books by Karen MacMurray

How to Become a Great Speaker

Historical Research for Novel Writers

WordPress Plugins for Writers

Books Coming Out Soon

How to Become a Best-Selling Author by Using Visual Media (It will cover how to leverage Pinterest, Instagram, Flickr, SlideShare, etc.)

Thank You!

I thank you for purchasing this ebook and would love to hear from you on how well you are doing. You can contact me at Karen@promote-your-book.com. You will find additional tips and articles there as well.

Before you go, I would like to ask for a "small" favor. *Could you please take a minute or two and leave a review for this book on Amazon?* Your feedback will help me to continue to write these types of book and make each one better.